Pascale Petit
The Zoo Father

D0132624

seren

seren
is the book imprint of
Poetry Wales Press Ltd
Nolton Street, Bridgend, Wales
www.seren-books.com

ISBN 1-85411-305-4

A CIP record for this title is available from
the British Library

*The publisher works with the financial assistance of the
Arts Council of Wales*

Cover Image: Nez Perce Horse Mask, Thaw Collection,
Fenimore Art Museum, Cooperstown, New York.
Photograph: John Bigelow Taylor, NYC

Printed in Palatino by
Bell and Bain Ltd, Glasgow

Contents

The Strait-Jackets

I lay the suitcase on Father's bed
and unzip it slowly, gently.
Inside, packed in cloth strait-jackets
lie forty live hummingbirds
tied down in rows, each tiny head
cushioned on a swaddled body.
I feed them from a flask of sugar water,
inserting every bill into the pipette,
then unwind their bindings
so Father can see their changing colours
as they dart around his room.
They hover inches from his face
as if he's a flower, their humming
just audible above the oxygen recycler.
For the first time since I've arrived
he's breathing easily, the cannula
attached to his nostrils almost slips out.
I don't know how long we sit there
but when I next glance at his face
he's asleep, lights from their feathers
still playing on his eyelids and cheeks.
It takes me hours to catch them all
and wrap them in their strait-jackets.
I work quietly, he's in such
a deep sleep he doesn't wake once.

Embrace of the Electric Eel

For thirty-five years, Father, you were a numb-fish,
I couldn't quite remember what it felt like

that last time you hugged me when I was eight,
just before you went away.

But when you summon me to your stagnant pool,
Dad, Papa, whatever I should call the creature

that you are, now you finally ask for my love:
do you think I've become strong as the horses

Humboldt forced into a stream
to test the voltage of Amazonian eels?

He had never witnessed
"such a picturesque spectacle of nature"

as those great eels clamped against the bellies
of his threshing horses, how their eyes

almost popped out and their manes stood on end.
Though the jolt alone did not kill them,

many were so stunned they drowned.
That's how it is, Father, when you open your arms

and press your entire length against my trunk.

Self-Portrait with Fire Ants

To visit you Father, I wear a mask of fire ants.
When I sit waiting for you to explain

why you abandoned me when I was eight
they file in, their red bodies

massing around my eyes, stinging my pupils white
until I'm blind. Then they attack my mouth.

I try to lick them but they climb down my gullet
until an entire swarm stings my stomach,

while you must become a giant anteater,
push your long sticky tongue down my throat,

as you once did to my baby brother,
French-kissing him while he pretended to sleep.

I can't remember what you did to me, but the ants know.

My Father's Voice

Because you refused to let me
record your voice
I've brought this parrot
all the way from Brazil,
the last speaker of a vanished tribe.
No-one understands him.
No-one speaks to him.
I'll leave him to perch beside your bed
until he can mimic
the hum of the oxygen machine
and those little phrases you repeat
to the girl who comes
and washes you in moisturising milk
and who cooks your meals.
You won't have to talk to him —
I know that's hard for you —
nor exercise him, he's used to a cage.
By the time I return, I expect him
to have learnt your language,
your sighs, your weeping even
and those gasps you make
on days when the air
is too heavy to breathe
even with supplementary oxygen.
And when you die,
I'll bring him to live in my home.
If I haven't seen anyone for weeks
I'll stroke his red and green feathers;
he'll remind me how precious each breath is
as I coax your voice from his beak.

The Fish Daughter

You tell me you loved fishing.
So I flop across your bed
like a giant pirarucú
and show you my armour-plated body
and my bonytongue.
You could make a rasp
from the teeth on my tongue,
with the things I'm saying,
and grate the past with it.
I open my cavernous mouth
so you can see how everything
is toothed: my jaws,
palate, pharynx — how you've caught
the biggest prize in the Amazon.

But when I go into the kitchen
and come back too quickly
and catch you peeing into a bottle
I know just what I've to do:
shrink myself to a tiny candirú,
the most feared fish in the river,
swim up your stream of urine
into your urethra, Father,
and wedge my backward-pointing barbs
deep inside your penis.

The Lungfish Father

I wish you could become a lungfish,
burrow underground
during the dry season,
pushing up through your tunnel
for gulps of air at first,
then sealing the entrance
with mud plugs.
You'd curl your tail around your head
and secrete a film of mucus
around your emaciated body,
remain in a state of torpor
while the earth bakes and cracks.
Safe in your cocoon,
you'd hardly breathe for months, years even,
until awakened by water.

Or if you were preparing
for the breeding season,
you'd grow a mysterious fringe
on your hind fin,
its filaments turning red
as they branch into
an extra breathing organ,
so that the lungfish father
can bring oxygen to his eggs
in the nest he alone
prepares and guards.

I wish I could grow
a breathing fringe
somewhere on my body,
to bring you oxygen
when you gasp to fill
your shrivelled lungs.
When all you can do
is sleep to ease the pain,
and all I can do
is sit on guard.
I'd secrete bubbles of oxygen
from my blood
and waft them over your mouth.

My Father's Lungs

All day I have been shrinking
and my father has been turning transparent.
There were moments when I held his soul
in a little tuft of eagle down,
while his dressing-gown and pyjamas
glowed like clothes of light.
We've drunk two bottles of champagne.
I've begun to see the entire
fauna of a forest in him.
It's like looking at a glass frog —
I can see through his clear blue skin
into his heart. But I'm no longer interested
in whether he loves me or not,
or if he really thought of me
every day of his years away.
I'm looking at those luminous trees
growing in his rib cage,
to replace his choked lungs.
I'm piercing his body membrane,
I'm so small now, it's like the skin of a sky
I can fly through, into his chest.
His breath is amplified all around me.
His lungs are white, shining
like X-rays in this twilight.
They branch in all directions
in a left and right garden,
separated by a stream.
His breath is separating into four winds —
the white, black, red and blue
that make coloured sounds, and sometimes
an octave of pure silver
as I watch an upper branch
burst into a swirl of starlight.

The grass is red, and wafts my feet
towards my next task:
I am gathering lungmoss for my pillow,
making a bed in his body.

Hummingbird

When I was a child I wanted you, Father,
to be a harpy eagle.
I wanted monkeys to be so scared of you
they'd plummet to the ground
at the merest shadow.
I waited for you to tear a sloth
from his branch and bring him to me,
rip off his limbs so I might eat
and grow my nine-foot wingspan.
Now that I've found you, I know
you're just a hummingbird.
I need an electron microscope
to see the new worlds
opening to me in your feathers,
how variable they are, depending on the light
and whether you allow me
to glimpse memories refracted in their sheen.
And when you talk to me in French,
I only understand part of what you say.
Your singing is mostly ultrasonic,
intense in frequencies beyond my imagining.
I know some notes hide deeper notes
though both may be sung together,
and that in your head, you compose
many other songs for me,
which you are not strong enough to sing.
Although you are tiny, you're brave enough
to attack and kill a pygmy owl,
that's how fiercely you battle
with your illness, and my questions.

And how do you see me?
Am I too big to take in?
You hover before the blur of my face
quite tamely. And once,
attracted to the salt in my sweat,
you licked my skin.

The Shawl

Just before she died my mother phoned
and told me she'd spent her life savings
on an antique shawl
which she was wearing
courtesy of Augusto Ruschi, hummingbird fancier.
"I'm wearing 8,000 hummingbirds" she said,
"can you hear them sing?"

I held the receiver against my ear,
obediently listening for ultrasonic cheeps.
"They sing 12,000 songs per day" she whispered,
her voice suddenly lowering as she buzzed
at an owl, then struggled in a spiderweb,
thousands of flowers still to visit,
her tongue probing the air,
her face disappearing in a funnel.

Motherfather

My mother says she might visit my father.
I picture him entangling her in his nasal tubes,
her running naked down the boulevard
taking him with her, carrying his oxygen cylinder.

They'd arrive at the apartment where we once lived
like conquistadores riding into Tenochtitlan,
the Aztecs mistaking them for centaurs
or flying deer snorting thunder and lightning.

I'm wondering how I can mount this beast
named Motherfather, scarred from so many battles,
as it gallops around my house
spitting gunpowder, setting my furniture on fire.

Self-Portrait as a Warao Violin

When they say "Go on, play your little girl"
he splashes rum on the walls and roof

of his house to get it drunk
and invites everyone.

Even the jaguar and monkey
stand on their hind legs

and dance together
as he rub-rubs my body.

He made me from a red cedar
in Delta Amacuro.

I'm half the size of civilised violins
but much more shapely.

The resonance chamber is my body,
the scroll my head.

I also have a waist and back.
When all the dancers have collapsed

he wraps me in an old shirt
and hangs me from the ridgepole.

No one but my father can touch me.
When he sleeps

the night breeze blows across my strings
and makes them hum.

King Vulture Father

I've spent all morning in the Ménagerie.
I sat in the Vallée des Rapaces
and stared at four *vautours papes* —
Sarcoramphus papas — surprised
by the beauty of these New World royals,
with their purple and coral heads
naked for thrusting into carrion,
and creamy neck ruffs to soak up liquids.
They reminded me of you — silk-pyjamaed
with your lambswool scarf,
moustache trimmed by the home help
who calls you His Majesty, as you issue
orders how to present your food
between crises in your breathing.
Even your cannula looks like an accessory
trailing from your nose like a vulture's wattle.
I'm waiting for you to start, Papa —
the king must feast first.

Do I remind you of the past
with my foul-smelling feathers?
How like your nestling I am, hissing
and vomiting when threatened.
What a putrid banquet I've swallowed,
keeping it in my crop to disgorge on your table.
Brother and I forced the lock of Mother's strongbox
to read her life's letters.
We ate the tongue and eyes first
then plunged our heads under the black leather lid
straight to the guts and arse.
Words wriggled like maggots about to sprout wings,
beetles with jewelled wing cases
crumbled to reveal your secrets.
We devoured letters she'd written to you but not sent,
the ink laced with poisons — our gastric juices
neutralised them. We were so hungry
for the truth, acid streamed from our beaks.

21

Self-Portrait as a Were-Jaguar

All morning I walked through the rain
until I'd seen every animal in the Ménagerie,
even the minibeasts in the microzoo.
However high I set the magnifier
I could not find excuses for you.
Like a sleepwalker, I glided down Raptor Way.
The Himalayan and king vultures
were old friends I could chat to
before I sat where I always sit
by the Fauverie, watching the jaguars mate.
The keeper smiled at me. It was Paris in Spring.
Where you met my mother. And raped her.

I passed the room where you first lived together
next door to the Jardin des Plantes.
Where you continued to rape her
while I lay in my flesh cage
listening with half-formed ears
to her cries, and your cries.
The male is a mature black jaguar.
He mounts the female, roars when he's finished.
She snarls from the barb on his penis.
This is how I spend my mornings, Father,
then I return to the hotel, prepare my mask.

You do not know that I am wearing this mask.
Please answer my questions, though you are dying.
The keeper gave me hairs from a jaguar's ears
to place in my ears so I can hear your thoughts.
I am wearing jaguar lashes around my eyes
so I can see into your heart.
Black quatrefoils are painted on my skin.
I have filed my incisors and canines.
I have painted the corners of my mouth black
to lengthen it into a maw.
I am wearing a thorn necklace.

The thorns are from the trunk of a tree
called "Black Jaguar's Claws Tree".
I found them in the hothouse.
After watching the jaguars mate
again and again, I went in there.
Some daughters turn into were-jaguars
in the forest of their fathers.
The thorns are infected with the worms of prey.
I made a worm-paste from the maggots
and smeared it on my arms to embrace you.
I am your putrefaction.

The Ant Glove

Dear Father, after Mother's death, after I'd read
    all your letters to her and her letters to you

and finally understood that I was the fruit of her rape,
    I walked into the forest.

The tribe I met there helped me write this letter
    preparing me as they would prepare a boy

who wanted to become a man.
    The elders raided nests of giant hunting ants

for three hundred shining black workers
    which they wove into the palm fibres of a glove,

their stinging abdomens pointing inwards.
    They blew on them to enrage them.

They painted my writing hand with black dye
    from the genipap fruit and thrust it into the glove.

I had to remain silent while the ants attacked.
    Can you smell the lemony scent of formic acid?

These words are dancing the Tocandeiro.
    I hope you're dancing as you hold my letter,

as I had to dance wearing the ant glove
    stomping my soles hard on the ground.

Afterwards I cut the stones from my feet.
    Afterwards I celebrated with a feast

biting off ant-heads to suck blood from their bodies
    until my lips and tongue were numb.

I hope you've sucked the blood from the words
　　that stung you. My hand is still swollen.

Are your fingers swelling as they stroke my signature?
　　Are your lips and tongue numb from kissing my kisses?

My hand is always in the glove, writing goodbye,
　　red and blue feathers flutter from my wrist.

A Wasps' Nest

"Only weak people see a therapist" he repeats.
And to stop myself from walking out

I send the warrior inside me
to search for a wasps' nest.

I'm answering back now, asking him if
there was anything he would have changed.

He's told me his mother was a bitch
and what the priests did in the boarding-school,

and I know that he punished my mother.
But he's run out of breath,

he's spitting in his jar.
A few wasps zoom into the air.

Then I see it — big as a head
and what I have to do is

hit the wasps' nest hard.
And keep on hitting it with my fist.

Inside there's a fat queen laying more stingers.
She's at the centre of the combs.

Out fly her workers, diving into my hair,
stabbing my face.

I hit harder. My fist swells.
Somewhere in the nest there's the room

where the queen will eat her daughters
when they challenge her,

there's the buzzing sound
Father hears when he can't breathe.

The sound I hear when I want to leave
and never come back. Not as a weakling.

I'm smashing the cell where Father lives.
The punching only stops when I pass out.

Trophy

After he shot you, my dear tormentor,
he made me take the gun, helped me
fire more shot into you.
I thought he had finished.
The burn in my palm felt numb.
When he severed your neck from your body,
again I thought it was finished.
But he parted your hair, started
to cut down the back of your scalp,
lifted the flesh from your skull.
And peeled back your face.
He sewed your hollow boneless skin
with a bamboo needle and palm-leaf fibre.
Skewered your lips with chonta pins.
He closed your eye holes, plugged
your nose and ears. Then he lit a fire.
He tipped your face upside-down,
turned it inside out and scraped off
the flesh with his machete.
Righted the bag that was you
and filled it with hot sand.
Placed your head in a pot
and kept bringing you to the boil,
removing your head each time
so your moustache and hair
remained attached. He tipped out
the cool and greasy sand then
ironed your skin with hot flat stones
until you were tough as tanned leather
and your pores released oil.
He swung your half-fried face by your hair.
There was a smell like supper cooking.

He put coarse pebbles inside you now,
they rattled, the oil bubbled out.
Your head shrank to the size of a fist.
You were cured, my perfect trophy father.
It was I who threaded red toucan feathers
from your miniature ears,
trailed white strings from your smile.

Father's Maps

The only maps I want now
are in my father's chest.

I'll unpick the old scar,
part the sawn ribs,

spread his lungs out flat
on the airport runway —

all fourteen thousand square feet
of air cells.

During the Eclipse

My father is breathing through
an oxygen machine,

only one branch left
in his lungs.

During the eclipse it flowers.
The flower has a corona

and for once, it's safe
to look at his dangerous light.

Dapple plays over his body
from the tree outside the window.

Crescent suns dance on his skin,
bathing him in lustral waters.

My Father's Body

As I sit here holding your hand
knowing that you were once a rapist,
I think how it isn't enough
just to shrink your head.
I could shrink your whole body
with the skills I learnt as a sculptor.
I'd use volcanic heat,
water from Fire River,
hot sand from its bed
and I'd sing to my materials.
They'd sing back, glowing.
Even Jivaro headhunters
would be shocked at how easily
I'd slit the sides of each limb,
peel the skin from your neck
and torso down to your feet.
How I'd discard your meat
and ask all my animals
if they were hungry.
The anaconda-canoe would carry
your organs to the feast
while I sewed your seams.
Then I'd boil your skin
and iron it with river flames.
I'd fill your body-sack with hot sand,
the badness would bubble out.
I wouldn't stop until
you'd shrunk enough to be my doll.
I'd hang you from a hook
and stare at my naked Papa —
your miniature penis
that couldn't hurt a mouse.
I'd take you to a part of the forest
where only children are allowed.
Walking there, I'd listen
to what your soul had to say.

When I arrived at the clearing
I'd lay you out. And stay
as the children gathered around
whispering, touching your tiny fingers.

My Father's Books

The moment of my father's death
his books slithered off their shelves,

they walked on their pages
like giant centipedes.

Or flew
like thousand-winged moon-moths

and landed on his body.
They wanted to read him

as he had read them
during his long illness,

often falling asleep,
his face on their faces.

And the words had hissed
like stick insects

flashing their wings
until he was awake again.

My emaciated father —
how often had I longed to pull open

his pink wings
furled under his shoulder blades

and read his sealed scripts,
my Spectre, my Touch Me Not.

But when I came
and kept vigil in his armchair

while he lay on his left ribs,
his back rolled around him like an exoskeleton,

all night I stared at his books
neat in their shelves.

And they stared back at me
through their spines

with star-insect eyes,
until his last breath.

Nesting

The day my father dies
    I lock myself in the Jewel Room
among my rare hummingbirds,
    my *oiseaux-mouches*.

I reject the Ruby-Topaz
    with his high-carat throat
and choose instead the female,
    so tame she drinks from my lips.

I offer her a leaf-bath
    then wrap her in her nightshirt,
wind cloth tape around her body
    pinning her legs and wings.

When she's quiet
    I give her the feeding bottle
which she accepts like a baby.
    And stow her in my coat pocket

for the ride to the mortuary.
    A man in white gown and gloves
guides us to the viewing room
    where my father's laid out,

a sheet tucked to his chin,
    his face a giant's
in the stark light.
    I unwind her dressings,

warm her in my hands,
    feed her nectar. She knows
exactly what to do, flies
    straight to his head,

selects only silver hairs
        to pull out and bring me
for safekeeping, a little cloud
        for my left pocket.

Back home, she uses her bill
        as a darning needle, stitching
the spiderwebs I supply
        to bind the translucent nest-cup,

presses herself against Father's hair,
        even slides her tongue
over stray ends. Before laying
        her first pure white egg.

The Wake

I've dressed you in your wedding suit
and laid you out in a field.

There's a frost and the birds are quiet,
the faintest sounds are amplified.

We can hear a spider weaving her web,
its low vibrations make every hair

on your face stand proud.
We eavesdrop on a baby mouse

noisily suckling in its nest, the cries
of stag beetles, lovesongs of flies.

That rabbit dreaming in its warren —
its snores and sighs sound

almost human but are higher-pitched,
like a ghost dreaming. I'd like

to protect you from the woodworm
already feeding on your coffin, their jaws

that creak like a ship in fog.
Let's pretend that you're on a voyage

and your vessel is this split hollowed
log I felled from virgin timber.

The last thing we hear before you leave
is the breath of a snail in the small hours.

The Horse Mask

Before the lid of your coffin
is screwed down, I slip in
my gift — a red horse mask,
folded between your heart
and the sheet. It will shine
in the dark, ready to be worn
by one of the wild horses of the sky.
That night I call them —
the white mare with a comet tail,
the black stallion splashed
with the Milky Way
and the brown horse made of soil,
trailing roots for a mane.
I call the fire-horse with volcanic hooves.
I ask one of them to lift you
over the gates of your death —
you're so light they could reach
the end of the universe before sweating.
I tell them what you have done.
I promise them apples
and a planet without people,
their own star-island.
All this for the brave one
who will wear the blood-mask,
who will lie in my father's grave
nuzzling his face to wake him.
All this for the strong one
who will bear your thin body
and fat soul far away and never return.

The Sea Father

I put on a mask and fins,
slide into the water.
Sunlight dances like flame

across the cave roof.
Two mating monk seals
stare straight at me.

I have to leave their black
eyes and thick whiskers
which remind me of my father,

and dive through a great arch
of vitrified lava, trailing
my comet tail of bubbles.

It takes an hour
to reach a darkness
only pierced by my lamp.

The pressure of almost
two vertical miles
pushes me against the floor

as my father once crushed
all light out of my mother
to make me.

I have to crawl over
waves of raw basalt
clutching his urn

until I find black smokers.
I must choose one
of these crooked chimneys

where life first began.
And pour his ashes
down its vent

back into earth's core.

The Whale Father

What are you doing down on the sea floor
three months after your death?
Blow out that long held breath,
burst through the blue skin of our planet.
Let the full weight of your fall
drag the sky down with you
with all its stars, my thunderer.
Slap your tail fluke
and I will follow in your wake.
I who wanted a leviathan for a father
will sink through the singing storeys of the sea.

See how I am laying out your big white skeleton
in perfect order on the deep-sea bed
as if it's an extinct species —
the double doorway of your massive mandibles,
vestigial pelvis, each intact vertebra.
I'll lie inside your spinal cord
breathing the last cylinder of my oxygen,
to watch this cuttlefish laying her eggs.
Soon, sea-mats will fur your ribs,
then brittle stars will suck the oils from your bones.

Self-Portrait as a Dugout Canoe

Once I was a white cedar in the forest.
The other trees parted like a curtain
and you stood before me, my new father.

You sang to me, dressed my branches
with ribbons, called me your little bride.
You ran your hands along my trunk

deciding where to cut. I said goodbye
to my leaves, to all the birds
that had once lived in my crown.

I toppled on my back. You stood
astride me, struck zigzag blows
with your axe until I was hollow.

You packed me with palm leaves
and lit a virgin fire inside me.
You said I was your celestial fiancée,

that the rims you'd carved were my legs,
stuck crossbeams in to stretch them.
Then your friends pushed me to the river

and you sang again, so I wouldn't
rise up and swallow you alive.
You spent your life navigating the swamps.

I waited and waited for you to die.
And when at last you drowned
I thought I was free of you.

But they decorated my stern and prow
with stars, and laid your corpse
inside me. Buried us together.

Self-Portrait as a Harpy Eagle

A man takes an inventory of your belongings
while I sit on the bed where you died,
next to your pyjamas and a surgical glove.
There's official time and then days
without lawyers, the oxygen turned off,
the arrival of the man who takes away
your machine and three cylinders.
There's the clothes fit for a supernatural,
lotions for cleaning angel-skin.
There are locked briefcases I have to saw through
with a serrated knife, diaries to be excavated
from boxes, dust forming veils on my face
and hands. I keep washing them.
I keep trying your suits on hoping one will fit.

I check in the mirror and see you behind,
your hair raised in a double crest,
surprised again at how small I am —
your little harpy, your eaglet.
I'm rocking myself into the quiet.
If I had down-feathers I'd fly to the nests
of the stars with lightning in my talons,
a mountain lake on my back.
If I had your corpse I'd give you a sky burial
and make flutes from your bones.
All I have are the addresses of hotels where you lived,
a map to study with my raptor eyes.
I am learning to magnify everything you've left —
raw potatoes in a pan sprouting trees.
In their crowns I can hear an eagle's sharp screams.

Amazonia

Into your room I came, tearing
the red wax seal on the door,
looking for tracks —
your body print on the sheet,
the pillowslip creased
from your last sleep,
feathers in the pillow
curled around your last dream.
My eye is an infrared lens
seeking heat in the blue
imprint of your cheek.
You asked me to stay here
after you died, so I'm lying
next to the new small fridge
and your urine bottles.

I'm hallucinating as any true
hunter should, having fasted
and lain here awake, chanting
to the spirits on the ceiling.
This is how I make the paint
ripple into a white forest canopy,
the trees burst into flower
and flowers turn into monkeys.
The day fauna stirs.
The red macaw shrieks
from your light fittings,
his plumes caught on the blades
of your air-conditioner.
Those tripwires you arranged —
one tug for on, two for off —
so you could control
the power from your bed,
are draped like mist-nets.

By noon, a mountain range
erupts from the plaster.
Come out, little animal
hiding in one of those cracks —
come out and let me tame you.

Auburn

It's an aurora that I'm holding —
my mother's hair, cut

and sealed in this envelope
to be opened after her death.

I can still see her head
sending out solar flares,

our dog's hair standing on end,
giving off crackling sparks.

We waited for the room to catch fire,
witnessed instead her polar night,

the curtains' dance, Mother
threatening the air with her scissors

ordering us to whistle
to bring the northern lights down.

They hissed, as if unwilling
to enter our house.

Then it arrived, that red aurora.
First the halo

that graced her baby photos,
then auburn ringlets,

swathes of a magnetic storm
with violet rays at its heart.

The sudden wreath of silver curls —
our carpet covered in fiery snow.

My Mother's Skin

When I remember her light-sensitive skin
I think of an octopus trying
to stuff itself into the smallest crevice
tentacle by tentacle, away from the children
in the aquarium hall. They keep
tapping on the glass. And I watch
knowing I'm that little girl and boy
and our mother has just been released
from another spell in the hospital.
They've given her ECT. Her luminous skin
flashes us a dazzling light show. We're scared
but curious as she waves her eight arms,
colours pulsing over her in electrical charges.

My Octopus Mother

She'd shoot out a cloud of liquid fire
if I visited her private tide-pool.

She went out only at night
to catch rats from the water's edge.

I have seen all her fright masks.
I have watched her tear herself to pieces

in an octopus rage
and eat five of her own arms.

I have waited with her for them to regrow.
She could make herself translucent

as a crystal vase
or opaque as the night-sky

studded with cold blue stars.
She could divide her body

into a yellow left side
and a purple right side.

Even after she died
her skin still mesmerised me,

paling at first to a pearly cream
then hours later, flickering with waves

of rose, topaz, ultramarine.
All her hallucinations passed

out of her like summer lightning —
a faint cobalt light, a last green spark,

the opal sheen of her eyes
before I closed them.

The Fish Mother

During a manic phase, she'd sometimes call me
— I'd know it was starting
by the shoals of glassfish,
the way they darted into my thoughts
as if I was a wrecked ship
and my phone had become a hydrophone
amplifying her voices.
Who understands the sounds fish make
to one another? Snorts, growls, grunts,
creaks like a balloon being pinched,
as they grate their teeth —
that's how Mother used to get.
A daughter can stand with her two feet
planted on the floor, gripping the receiver,
but their songs will still
vibrate through her bones.
What my mother said in those drowned
monologues was never in human speech.
She spoke through light, she rubbed
her voicebox with the yellow liquid
from a rat-fish's light gland
and shone sky-blue for hours.
She dangled her luminous lures
like a deep-sea angler-fish,
on flaps of winking skin, and
I always took her bait, engulfed
by one of her fish mouths.
And always, below the realm of twilight
— a world of perpetual silence,
a sudden blackout of mirror-scales,
the arrival of a shoal of star-eaters.

The Dolphin Father

I've been to Belém, wandered
through its *Ver-O-Peso* market —

see-the-weight stalls
so packed they blocked out the sun.

I picked up a bottle of perfume
containing a pickled baby boa,

saw large rubber monkeys masturbating.
And a jar of jaguars' testicles.

Then an old *curandeiro* led me
to a back stall, promised a miracle cure.

He unwrapped "play toys" from damp newspapers:
dried dolphin eyes, a dolphin's pink penis.

He told me to look through the left eye
for the face of my first love.

I had to grind the penis into a paste
mixed with pubic hairs and menstrual blood.

And this is how I made you rise, Papa,
from your room on the river floor,

dressed in a white suit, stingray shoes.
Your name was *boto*, enchanter, dancer.

You whispered: "A girl who has sex
with a dolphin dies of pleasure."

51

Self-Portrait as a Yanomami Daughter

I've built a rainforest shelter,

painted *hekura* on the walls —
my only visitors, these helper-spirits.

I haven't been out since you died.
Like a good Yanomami daughter

I've kept our fire alight.
Your body made it burn so fiercely.

My hair singed as I raked
the embers for all your bones

to grind to a black powder.
When I finished, the *hekura* spoke.

They told me to shave my hair
and braid it into a belt,

bind it tight around my waist
the way you used to hold me, Father,

when you turned into a demon
and tore me with your penis.

This is how Night was made,
my thighs sticky with star-blood,

my mouth flooded with moonseeds.
Now, I wear a child's necklace

threaded with toucan beaks.
I shake my rattle,

stamp my clapping stick.
I pour your ashes into plantain soup.

The first sip makes me retch,
then I learn to like the taste.

The Musical Archer

All my life I have been carrying
a river on my back.

I lay it down in the house of silence.
I bring out the old instruments:

the deerskull with its murmuring tone,
the howler monkey skin drum,

my belt of snail shells and oilbird legs
that clatter and break the house's spell.

Sometimes, I want to remember my father
playing his musical bow.

Its sharp, metallic throb,
more insistent than the insects,

is how these memories start.
He used to pluck the string for hours

to lull his prey into a trance.
When the animals came, how quickly

he turned his lure to a weapon
and shot them. When I approached,

he pulled me onto his lap
and filled me with hot arrows.

He trained those darts to vibrate
inside me like hummingbirds over flowers.

Time also hovered. Its dragonfly wings
are this cool breeze on my face.

Even now, as I bathe in the river —
all the little arrows he released

are aroused. They dance to his music,
spread concentric ripples through the water.

The Magma Room

Then his window turned to quartz crystal
and his curtains to rock.
I was back in the magma chamber
of my childhood
               in my father's bedroom.

He'd punched a crater in my chest
and we'd both fallen in
then resurfaced, burnished,
the heat almost melting my bones,
the sheets glowing red, then
               bursting into flame.

My face pressed into the lava pillow
would always leave a mask
as he pushed further into me.
And when I tried to pull away,
the stone face I now had,
stared at the ceiling
               and saw it bubble.

My long black hair
flowed down me in rivers of fire
which he kept stroking and twisting
               until the roots tore.

I slipped into a molten darkness,
down to a white core
where I was numbed.
A doctor woke me
on the cool kitchen table.

Over forty years have passed
since I buried that night
under clouds of volcanic ash.

But when you ask me what I remember —
all I say is his smell,
         like a stone lining in my nostrils.

My Father's Clothes

During the last nights of my father's life
I took refuge in his wardrobe

in the silence of its forest, among clothes
I had never seen him wear,

that he had not worn for years.
Silk shirts so light on their hangers

like the ghosts of tree people,
moonbeam blue and mist green

— all his pristine mornings
waiting for me to breathe on them

and perform my curing ceremony.
Suits of shining black and midnight blue,

fabrics I had to feel, summoning
his memories from their fibres,

expecting thorns to scratch my skin,
as if they required my blood.

Coats taking root in the wardrobe floor
like buttresses of great ceibas,

requesting me to crouch inside
their hollowed hearts, go with him

on his last walk.
Coats that had drunk his sweat

as he struggled up his apartment steps
dragging his portable oxygen,

that year when he could still
taste rain-feathers on his tongue,

his lungs squeezed to their roots,
the coats loosening their grip

as he grew thinner.
All my life I'd yearned

to press my face into these clothes,
had imagined a row of costumes

for him to disappear in:
a raven feather cloak or condorskin robe.

And to reappear in:
a bark cape or snow owl waistcoat.

And there, between the buttresses —
the last pair of shoes he wore

nestling together like sleeping deer,
traces of mud on their hides.

THE VINEYARD

A Parcel of Land

This is the last piece of wild land,
left to me by accident, by dream.
I want to unwrap it like a parcel,
a pass-the-parcel in newspaper,
promised but always snatched away.
Some at the party hold it to their ear
and hear cicadas singing to a mate
in another parcel in another game,
and pass it quickly like a bomb
or shake it until it rattles.
Sometimes the newsprint smudges
and the paper's black with petroleum rain.
And sometimes the parcel's thrown
and threatens to fly off like a magician's dove.
 I sit on the floor, expecting it to be hollow
— a cave in its mountainous layers.
Then the music stops and it's in my lap
wearing one thin atmosphere.
I open it as an angel might part the clouds,
receiving a gift from her dead god.
To remove that last blue tissue
I grow the fingers of all the hungry
and my land scratches me with its brambles.

Landowners

What does it mean to own a half-hectare?
I stood on the bank of the stream

and asked the stones and the pools:
how deep do my boundaries extend,

through how many seams of mantle?
How high? Up to where the indigo sky

is feathered with black?
For a full hour the cork oaks were silent

while I questioned each leaf.
Then a voice came from the branch

and I saw two kingfishers.
Tchi chee, they said, *kwee kwee*,

and I knew they were speaking
the lost language of the land,

that this estate I'd inherited
was theirs.

Their costumes confirmed it —
wings of the intensest sun blue

shimmering like atmospheres
over the bronze earths of their bodies.

Reverse Vineyard

I climb over the low wall.
Every stone is warm.
It's been sunny all night,
like those negatives left unprinted
for thirty years, everything is in reverse —
the orange sky, white vines
with lilac leaves.
Halfway up the steep path
our vanished hut comes into view,
wobbling in the haze
like a photo in the developing tray.
But it's back to front and left to right;
the lab's got it wrong.
No matter, this is my only chance.
Maman is at the door,
cheeks tilted for a goodnight kiss.
I wish her good morning
even though her face looks crooked.
I can mend it with these newborn eyes
that first see upside down
then correct the world.
"Sit down" I order,
cradling her shoulders with my arm
so that neither of us knows
who is mother or daughter.

The Songs of Insects

(for my mother)

This is your sleep-cure,
    your wild acre —

move in closer, with micro-camera
    and amplifier.

Thrust a crystal microphone
    into the vines.

Shine mirrors on the boldest singers —
    those gladiators and shield-bearers

and don't forget to register
    the pulses of silence

between each chirp.
    Now we are listening to the courtship

dance of the days
    before your illness,

before the radioactive iodine,
    the lithium poisoning —

none of this has happened yet.
    Let's talk about wings — how one

has a file with teeth
    and the other a scraper —

that they rub together to make music.
    Let's whisper about cricket legs with ears,

their membranes vibrating with your dreams.
    Though the stone huts are ruins,

we can lie under the olive tree.
    I'll cut you a path

through thirty years' bramble
    and join you at dusk,

much too excited to sleep.
    The night songs are waiting for us.

The snowy tree cricket
    stretches his pale green body

and diaphanous wings.
    Shyly and secretively he's calling.

His song is an audible stillness,
    a purr, a baby's breathing.

If moonlight could be heard
    it would sound like this.

The Second Mazét

Do you still dream of your mazét —
    the second one
        that has vanished?

Although it's small,
    let's open its thirty doors —
        one for each year of your madness.

Let's open the shutters
    and let the curious light
        see you typing,

in larval languages,
    thirty hornets' nests
        of letters to your family.

Over the roof, the walnut tree
    ripens. I crack open
        its tiny skulls,

try not to break each shrivelled brain:
    the manic-depressive, schizophrenic,
        the one no doctor can name.

Here come the shakes, the runs,
    the sweats. Oh,
        but they can't get the dose right.

While you sleep, I'll harvest our grapes —
    a vintage better than any pill.
        I'll sweep the dead leaves

from the streambed, and lay
    stones where crayfish can breed.
        We have everything you need

for a healthy second life.
    I've hung a cricket in a red cage
        for luck, over your grave.

Mazét: Languedoc for drystone hut

A Stone Face

In the museum at Lodève
I found a fragment
of a woman's face
embedded in a stalagmite.
They called her "The Howler"
from the Clamouse Caves.
I thought she was you.
And I was the child the other side
of the limestone plateau,
launching toy boats to reach you
along the fast-flowing
subterranean river.
And I was the corpse
that came floating later,
through the razor-edged corridors.
I passed The Bride's Bouquet,
drank earthmilk,
was almost trapped in a giant geode.
As I arrived,
the water
cleaned me of all guilt.

And I came home,
through those crystal chambers,
to my stone mother.

Home Was a Cyanide Bottle

Home was a cyanide bottle.

We burrowed into the cork
like little beetles

adapting to the very poison
used to kill us.

Sometimes we were flies
pinned on the chairs

of Mother's living room.
Our eyes budded wings.

And sometimes we were firebugs
with blistered neckplates,

holes in our armour.
Our feelers grew leg-parts.

Each night a new accident
in the nuclear family,

the air radiant
with its imploding moods.

And nobody came
to shut down the reactor.

Woman-Bottle

(after Picasso)

They have bottled me and painted
my happy-portrait on the front.

I'm almost opaque
like milk opal some mornings

when sunlight strikes
a prism in my neck.

I think I may be kind then,
hold wine from the mother-vine.

By evening, all is ocean dark.
My fluids distort their voices.

Are they afraid to uncork me?
They should be. A storm's

been circling inside my head
for centuries.

Can they see my real eyes?
They are the eyes of hurricanes

that no-one will drink
however reckless they become.

At the bottom of my interior,
in silt, a shark's tooth

waits to be poured
into the last drinker's mouth.

Then I will kiss him
with a glass's cold lips.

My Mother's Tablets

I made a model of the vineyard
from your leftover pills,

dry wall terraces
from all the etiolated tablets

they'd tested on you.
I ground lithium salts for the soil,

used what you'd called
horsepills and donkeypills

to build our two stone huts —
the front one and the hidden one

in the back corner
infested by the black rats of depression.

I planted vines of your hair,
with roots from your scalp.

For my first visit to your grave
on this cold Welsh hill

I place not flowers
but this model of the Midi,

then let loose
a box of mole crickets

to burrow into the ground
and trill in their tunnels

all the manic night,
as if Earth herself is singing.

The Snake Dress

In the old olivewood box
you'll find a dress sewn
from the skins of grass snakes,
the ones that left their ghosts
on our vineyard walls.
Open the moss-lined lid,
shake out the folds
from their beds of brown leaves.
Unwrap my gift long
as our dry stream
and sheer as moonlight.
See how I've stitched the seams
with spider silk
stronger than steel,
so that each silver stripe
and diamond scale
is intact, your hands
soft as the southern breeze.
Let me clean the earth
from your face, my mother,
with this vial of walnut water.
And as you slip the dress
over your head — remember
how the snakes' eyes
go milky just before sloughing,
then clear, as the skin
loosens around their lips,
how they rub their sides
against stones before
turning themselves inside out.

Acknowledgements

Many thanks to the editors of the following, in which some of these poems first appeared: *Ambit, Boomerang, The Exeter Competition Anthology, 1999, The Forward Book of Poetry, 2001* (Forward Publishing, 2000), *Parents* (Enitharmon, 2000), *Poetry Quarterly Review, Poetry Wales, Quadrant* (Australia), *Rattapallax* (USA), *The Rialto, Wasafiri*.

Special thanks to Robert Minhinnick for publishing 22 of these poems in *Poetry Wales* and to Les Murray for publishing 17 in *Quadrant*.

"The Strait-Jackets" was shortlisted for the Forward Best Single Poem Prize in 2000. "My Father's Voice" was a prize-winner in the 1999 Peterloo Poetry Competition.

I am very grateful to the Society of Authors for a bursary in 1999, to London Arts for a New London Writers' Award in 2001, and to the Arts Council of England for a Writers' Award in 2001.

I would like to thank all those who have assisted with these poems, particularly Moniza Alvi and Scott Verner.

I am also indebted to Nathaniel Hawthorne for his description of the snowy tree cricket.